Contents

Getting started...

Your checklist for a happy healthy pet

[ ] Cage or gerbilarium
[ ] House or bedroom
[ ] Woodshavings, wood-
    based litter or fine peat
[ ] Pet bedding
[ ] Gerbil food
[ ] Food bowl
[ ] Water bottle

[ ] Mineral stone
[ ] Vitamin supplement
[ ] Bottle brush
[ ] Tubes & wooden toys
[ ] Gnawing sticks or chews
[ ] Gerbil treats
[ ] Cage disinfectant

Useful books

[√] Good Pet Guide: The Gerbil
[ ] Pet Friendly: Gerbils

Introduction

1. Gerbil

Gerbils are great pets. They are social animals that have a gentle and affectionate nature. Their home takes up little space and they only require a small amount of your time for feeding and cleaning.

The Latin name for a gerbil is *"meriones unguiculatus"*, which means *"clawed warrior"*, a reference to a Greek warrior called *Meriones* who went into battle wearing a helmet adorned with boar's teeth.

As its Latin name suggests, the gerbil has been shaped by its natural environment into a true desert survivor. In the wild they can survive with little water or food because of their ability to re-absorb liquids *(leaving highly concentrated urine and dry feces)*. This and the fact they do not lose water through sweat, make the gerbil the king of the desert!

In captivity they are cute and inquisitive pets. They can even be taught to climb up your shoulder or even to sit on your head!

Gerbils are lots of fun to own and their interactions and energetic antics will entertain you for hours.

"My name means 'Clawed Warrior' in Latin!"

2. Origins & habitat

The gerbils natural environment is the desert. They live with high temperatures, little rainfall and only small amounts of food.

Because of the temperatures above ground in the desert, gerbils have evolved into excellent burrowers. They dig down into the ground to find cooler surroundings and to find safety when they feel threatened by birds of prey. In the wild, a gerbils burrow can become a complex system of tunnels with sleeping or rest areas and food storage chambers.

Unlike most desert animals, the gerbil is not strictly nocturnal and will spend time awake during the day and night.

The gerbils origins lie in Mongolia and North Eastern China. The domestic gerbil as we know it, is a descendent of the *Mongolian gerbil*.

They became popular subjects for scientists in the 1950s. With its gentle nature and cute appearance, it wasn't long before they were sought after pets across Europe and the U.S.

3. Life span

Life expectancy can vary greatly with gerbils, but typically single gerbils live between 2-3 years, whilst groups live for about 4-5 years.

China

India

MONGOLIA

Perfect pet?

4. Great pets

A gerbil is a highly social and gentle small rodent that is roughly between a rat and a mouse in size.

An average adult will grow between 6-10 inches (15- 25 cm) including its tail. The tail will normally be half the overall length of the body.
A healthy adult gerbil should weigh around 2.4 oz (70 g) which means they are very light to pick up and handle. Because of this, always supervise children if they handle the gerbil and ensure they do not squeeze or handle them roughly.

Fun to watch

Gerbils are curious little animals. They love to explore their surroundings, digging and creating tunnels, climbing, jumping and chewing up anything they can get their teeth into! They are not easily scared, so they won't mind you getting close to watch them as they play and go about their business of creating burrows and hide outs.

Don't leave me alone!

Gerbils, like many other small animals, love the company of their own kind. They are naturally sociable and prefer to live in groups than on their own. Females are more quarrelsome than males, but when males fall out, it tends to be more vicious.

Whatever you decide, make sure that your cage is big enough for the group you have. Although gerbils like company, they still need their own space at times. Cramped conditions can lead to frustration and fighting or even aggression toward their handler.

5. Quality time!

A gerbil can really be a fun pet to own. They rarely bite, so as they become used to your touch, they will be happy to interact with you.

They are fun little pets to watch and with a little training and the occasional treat, can be taught to come to you every time you approach the cage.

Important!

Never use cedar shavings! They can cause respiratory problems in gerbils.

Varieties

6. What do you want?

The first thing you need to think about is what you want from your pet gerbil?

How many do you want? Are you going to buy gerbils of the same sex, or are you going to breed them?

7. How many?

As with many small animals, gerbils are very sociable with their own kind.

They love the company of other gerbils and can become quite unhappy if left alone.

If you are not planning to breed your gerbils, then a pair of females is probably your best option. Two males may fight with each other, especially as they become more mature. Whichever you choose, try to purchase your gerbils together when young. This way, they should become life-long companions that play, groom and sleep together.

Never try to introduce a new gerbil to an existing colony. If an unfamiliar gerbil is introduced, it may be attacked or even killed! *(see p23 for Introductions).*

8. Colors

There are many colors of gerbils available, from light cream to almost black in color.

They may have patches of color in a different shade to the base coat. These are known as *'marked'* gerbils.

9. Gerbil relatives

Gerbils are often called *jirds,* which is taken from an Arabic word that means *'large desert rodent'.*

If you love gerbils, then you may also like some of their close relatives. Other species of gerbils include the *Pallid Gerbil, Persian Jird,* the *Fat-tailed Duprasi* and *Shaw's Jird.*

Top tips

Even though gerbils are sociable with other gerbils, they may not always be happy to see a new arrival into their group. Sometimes it may be necessary to keep gerbils apart in separate cages *(see p23 'introductions').*

You should be careful to wash your hands before and after handling gerbils from separated cages. The scent you carry from one cage to the next can be threatening and may lead to distrust.

10. Species

Unfortunately, different species of gerbils do not mix (ie. Jirds do not mix with standard gerbils).

If you really want to have more than one kind, you should house them in another cage. Mixed cages will almost always lead to fighting.

Choosing your gerbil

11. Male or female?

Sexing a gerbil can be quite tricky, especially when they are young. Use the following tips to help:

Top tips

Adult gerbils measure about 6- 10 inches (15- 25 cm) in length from head to tail.

The tail is used to aid balance and will help them to leap and turn.

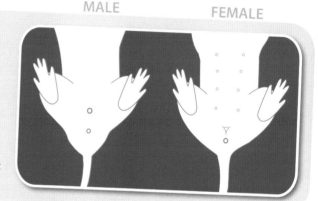

- → Male gerbils have a darker colored scrotum, located near the base of their tail.

- → The difference between the anus and the genital papilla is greater in a male.

- → Females have nipples.

- → If your still having trouble sexing your gerbil, ask your pet shop assistant for help.

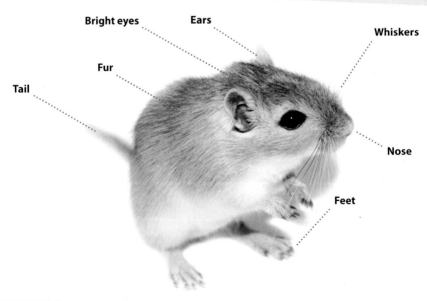

Tail

Bright eyes

Ears

Fur

Whiskers

Nose

Feet

12. Know your gerbil

A few things to look out for when choosing your gerbil :-

→ Eyes

Always make sure the gerbils eyes are large, bright and shiny. Runny or dull eyes are a clear signal of a sick animal.

→ Ears

A sign that there is a problem with a gerbils ear is that it will tilt its head or start spinning in circles. If a gerbil is seen shaking its head a lot or yawning, there may be an infection in the middle ear *(Take it to the vet to be checked out)*.

→ Teeth

Healthy gerbil teeth are yellow in coloration and not white! Gerbil teeth grow for the full extent of their life, so checking for length and alignment of teeth is very important! Top incisors should sit just in front of the bottom incisors but not overlap or grow at different angles. Gerbils are born to chew. This chewing is in fact perfectly natural behavior and is key to keeping the teeth worn down. If your gerbils teeth grow too long, it will starve!

→ Nose

Your gerbils nose should above all be clean, free from discharge, scabs and hair loss. Steer clear of one that has a sore, red or bleeding nose. It is an indication of an infection or an allergy to their current bedding.

→ Tail

The tail should be full and furry. It should be a similar length to the body, with a florish of fur at the end.

→ Coat

A healthy gerbils fur should be clean and soft. Dry, rumpled or ruffled fur is a sign of a sick animal.

→ Curiosity

Gerbils are naturally curious and once used to you, should perk up and enjoy your contact. Be patient to build up this relationship slowly and gently so that your gerbil trusts you.

→ Depression

Even a healthy gerbil can get depressed if its left alone too much. If the gerbil then perks up when handled and his eyes and fur look fine, then its most likely a healthy animal that has just become lonely. Groups of gerbils rarely show any signs of depression.

Housing your gerbil

13. Gerbilariums

The most common type of gerbil cage has a plastic base and a rigid wire top. This is commonly known as a *gerbilarium*.

The wire top of the cage can be easily removed from the plastic base. This makes it far easier to get the gerbil out to clean the inside. The plastic base can be deeply filled with wood shavings allowing your gerbils to dig tunnels. The clear sides also allow you to watch your little pets as they dig and play.

The upper wire level normally supports a platform level, or sometimes two. This is the climbing area. You can attach your water bottle, tubes and other toys here. Gerbilariums are practical, strong and reasonably priced.

14. Homemade cages

Some people opt to make their own cage. Homemade cages can easily be made from wood, wire mesh and Perspex. The base, back and sides are normally made from wood with a Perspex front panel. Finally the top is made from wire mesh with hinges and a securing latch.

The disadvantage with homemade cages is that they are usually solid on the sides and back which doesn't allow you to see your gerbil, unless looking from the front or above. If you do decide on the DIY option, make sure there are no sharp or rough edges and no gaps that your gerbil can escape through.

15. Aquariums

Some people use aquariums to house their gerbils.

Aquariums are draft proof and relatively cheap. They make ideal cages for pregnant gerbils, nursing mothers and baby gerbils.

It is always best to ensure a lid is fixed to an aquarium. The lid will ensure nothing is accidentally dropped on the gerbil, and will also help prevent the gerbil from escaping. A wire mesh top is preferable to a solid lid with air holes as this prevents the build up of condensation.

Gerbils love to dig, so an aquarium provides an ideal environment for them to do this if filled with a deep layer of wood shavings.

Pushing tunnels or cardboard tubes down into the sawdust will encourage the gerbil to dig deep and burrow under the surface.

The gerbil food guide

16. Food glorious food

It is preferable that you use a good premixed gerbil food. It will give your pet the perfect combination of vitamins, minerals, protein and bulk.

Sunflower seeds are very high in fat, and for obvious reasons are fattening to your gerbil.

It would be wise to pick out the sunflower seeds and feed them by hand to your gerbils over the day. This has the effect of ensuring that no single gerbil can eat the majority of the sunflower seeds and get too fat. It also helps with taming and bonding with your gerbils.

1. Sunflower seeds
2. Gerbil chew
3. Carrot wood roll
4. Broccoli
5. Apple
6. Water bottle

1.

17. Treats

Treats are just that, treats, and should be fed sparingly.

Your gerbil will love the ones listed below and they all have good health benefits. You should however be careful to limit treats to about 2-3 times a week in small amounts:-

→ **Brazil nuts**
→ **Whole-grain bread** (plain or toasted)
→ **Cereal** (plain, low sugar, no corn)
→ **Egg** (hard boiled)
→ **Flax seeds**
→ **Lentils**
→ **Meal worms**
→ **Peanuts** (unsalted)
→ **Rice** (wholemeal cooked)
→ **Walnuts**

2.

3.

4.

5.

Top tips

Suitable safe foods:

→ Broccoli
→ Parsley
→ Strawberry
→ Watercress
→ Apple
→ Chickweed
→ Basil
→ Carrot

Poisonous foods to avoid:

→ Pineapple
→ Buttercup
→ Onion
→ Potato
→ Poppy
→ Aubergine
→ Garlic
→ Rhubarb
→ Cucumber
→ Daffodil
→ Lemon
→ Tomato

18. Fruit & veg

Gerbils come from a dry climate and should only have a restricted amount of fresh produce, you shouldn't exceed 2 portions a week.

You must take care to not overfeed as this can cause your gerbil an upset stomach or diarrhoea.

Introduce new food types gradually to your gerbil, they will need time to get accustomed to a different diet.

Do not feed too many types of food at once and try not to make the portions too large. Be especially careful if the gerbil has never had fresh food before.

6.

19. Water

Your gerbil will require constant access to water.

A dish should not be used to hold water as it will quickly become contaminated with cage debris and urine, which will inevitably result in sick gerbils. Water bottles are a much better choice, especially ones with ball-bearings in the tube, which lead to less leakage.

Remember, provide fresh water daily, not just when the bottle is empty!!

Play time

20. Keep fit!

In its natural environment a gerbil may travel several miles in one day as they forage for food.

Your gerbil will need a way to use this natural energy, so you should make sure that the environment you create for them has places to climb and explore, somewhere to dig and ideally an exercise wheel where they can run to their hearts content. Exercise will lead to your gerbil being happier and healthier. Try to steer clear of wired wheels as they are bad for your gerbils feet. A silent spinner would be a better choice.

1. Exercise wheel
2. Runner ball
3. Tunnel block
4. Plastic tube system

Note. Not all gerbils like exercise wheels, so don't be worried if they don't want to use it. Just make sure they have a way to exercise.

1.

21. Boxercise...

When you have a group of gerbils together in a cage, it is not unusual for them to partake in a little sparring match.

Gerbil *'boxing'* matches normally take place between young gerbils *(pups)* and are not at all violent. They normally involve some chasing and wrestling, but no biting. At the end of the game, the winner normally ends up holding the loser down and grooming it.

These boxing matches are quite normal behavior and help to strengthen the social group.

Runner Ball

Balls are also great fun for your gerbil. A hamster ball will be great, though you must supervise them during their exercise as they may escape.

2.

22. Tunnel time!

Gerbils love tunnels. In the wild, their habitat will be a series of complicated tunnels and as a pet, their love of tunnels will not change.

Your gerbil will create tunnels from anything it can. If you put wood chippings in to a minimum depth of about 4 inches (10 cm), the chances are, it will have a tunnel running under it in no time.

If you're using card toilet or kitchen roll tubes, please make sure that the card is safe for your pet. Some card tubes have glue that can be harmful to your gerbil. There are several vegetable fibre paper tubes available that are not only fun for your gerbil to chew, but tasty too.

If you really want to see your pet scurrying around enjoying tunnels, the best way is to buy tubes, or a cage that already has some, from your pet store. Most of these tubes are made from safe, clear plastic and can be designed into different systems every few days to keep you and your gerbil amused!

Be careful that the tubes are tough enough as gerbils can chew through some plastics and escape.

3.

4.

Top tips

Fighting

Serious fighting can occur, especially between male gerbils.

Unlike play fighting, this is very serious and should be stopped as soon as possible.

It may often start as a staring match, followed by frantic chasing. At the height of these fights, gerbils will pounce upon each other biting at the face and neck. These bites can draw blood, and if they are not stopped, the fight may be fatal.

Be careful when intervening, use a cloth or gloves to avoid being bitten yourself!

Health

23. Good health

To ensure your gerbil remains in good health, make sure that their diet has an adequate intake of vitamins and minerals, through a fresh, high quality diet.

24. Wood gnaws

Wood gnaws are available in pet shops or you can provide your own by supplying the gerbil with a piece of apple branch.

These provide the gerbil with something on which to gnaw in order to keep its teeth trim.

Did you know?

Did you know the word 'rodent' is derived from the Latin word 'rodere' which means 'to gnaw'.

One of the best indicators of good health with a gerbil is bright and sparkly eyes.

25. Health problems

➔➔ Improper diet

Did you know that many problems in gerbils can be attributed to an improper diet?

Feeding gerbils too much fresh food can result in diarrhoea. This unpleasant symptom can also happen if your gerbils eat food that has gone bad. It's a good idea to keep a sick gerbil on dry foods for a couple of days *(If the symptoms persist, take your pet to a qualified veterinarian).*

➔➔ Respiratory problems

Gerbils are vulnerable to respiratory problems, particularly the common cold.

Cold symptoms can include sneezing, hacking, wheezing and a runny nose or eyes. Gerbils suffering from colds will shiver and huddle up together in an attempt to keep themselves warm. Keep the affected individual in a warmer area of the house *(If the symptoms persist take your pet to a qualified veterinarian).*

➔➔ Sore nose

Gerbils can sometimes get sore/ bleeding or crusty noses due to an allergy to its bedding *(in the event of this change the bedding. If problem continues consult your veterinarian).*

They are also vulnerable to colds. The symptoms will be the same as in humans. It can even be humans who pass the cold to the gerbil. So if you are taken ill, stay away from handling your gerbils until you're feeling better.

➔➔ Eye Infections

Gerbils are forever digging and burrowing around.

It is not uncommon for sand, bedding or dirt to get trapped behind the nictitating membrane, or the third eyelid *(found at the inner corner of the eye).* If your pet keeps scratching its eye, or you find loss of fur around the eye, consult your veterinarian.

• •

Other things to look out for aside from the health issues mentioned are lethargy, a dull or uneven coat, and a crouching posture. *(If you think one of your gerbils is ill, take your pet to a qualified veterinarian).*

➔➔ Parasites

Gerbils are prone to some parasitic infestations.

Mites, for example, can cause itchy lesions and loss of fur in affected gerbils.

If your pet is constantly scratching and biting himself or has dry skin, dandruff or hair loss, fleas or lice may be the cause.

Consult your veterinarian for treatment.

Cage care

26. Home sweet home

Gerbils are easy to look after. Their small bodies have evolved to survive on limited amounts of food and water, they hardly waste any body fluid and as such only excrete concentrated urine and dry feces.

If their cage has an abundance of absorbent peat and/or wood shavings, the animals can live in clean environment for quite some time *(see p17 for more details on cleaning).*

Check their food on a daily basis for spoilage or staleness. Food should be changed at least every 3 days to prevent your gerbils eating food that has lost it's nutrients. Any uneaten fresh food such as fruit or vegetables should be removed the following day and water changed daily.

1.

27. Safety first

Gerbils need bedding to absorb urine. They will also use the bedding for digging around in. As mentioned before, the gerbil doesn't urinate that much, so it doesn't have the need for perfumed bedding.

2.

If cleaned regularly, your gerbils cage should never smell. Fill your tank 1/3 full with bedding. They really love piling up their bedding, and burying their food in it.

If you are breeding though, two inches of the recommended bedding should be sufficient.

Shredded plain paper will work as gerbil bedding, but be prepared for the cage to smell a bit sooner than if the recommended beddings are used.

A good quality herbage hay is always enjoyed as well as half a kitchen roll with the paper still attached.

Important!

DO NOT use shredded paper with any sort of newsprint on it, as it is toxic to gerbils.

1. *'Snak Shak'* edible home
2. Kiln-dried pine shavings
3. *'Creepy Castle'* cage
4. Dust bath

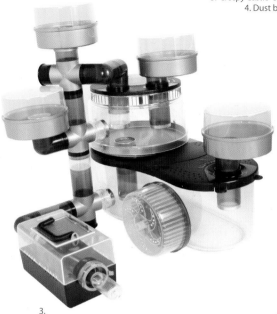

3.

Top tips

Making space

While you are carrying out your daily gerbil house keeping, pop your gerbil into a holding cage or exercise ball. ✓

28. A clean home is a happy home!

Here are some tips to help you make sure you keep your gerbils cage clean and hygienic:

Every day:
Remove all stale food and check the water bottle.

2 to 3 times a week:
Provide a dust bath. This is an important way of cleaning for your gerbil. Try placing a dish of Chinchilla dust in the cage for them to roll around in. Remove the dish after about 2 to 3 hours.

4.

Once a week:
Check for dirty bedding, remove and replace.

Once a month:
Remove all bedding. Thoroughly sweep out all the soiled bedding. Rinse with warm water and small animal detergent and wait until dry.

Alternatively, wipe all around with small animal cage cleaning wipes. Refill with clean bedding.

Handling your gerbil

29. Don't rush

Most gerbils in your local pet shop will be about 6 weeks old. If you are having a gerbil from a breeder, it is a good idea to wait until it is at least 6 weeks. This gives the gerbil time to develop social skills and bond with other gerbils. Your breeder will also introduce the gerbils to human handling.

Once you've brought your gerbil home, give them a few hours to get used to their new home. Next, place your hand into their tank and let them familiarize themselves with your scent. It's quite normal for you to get a gentle nip as they explore and examine your hand. This shouldn't be seen as an aggressive act, they're actually *"tasting"* you, in an attempt to figure out if you're edible. It won't hurt!

Hand training, if approached in the correct way, will prove to be effective and easy. Just remember to be patient with your gerbils and move at a slow pace *(you don't want to frighten your gerbil as it will take a while for it to trust you again)*.

Every morning while you're feeding your gerbils, remove all of their sunflower seeds from their feeding bowl and keep these seeds separately near the tank. Occasionally throughout the day, place a couple of these sunflower seeds in the palm of your hand and try to coax them to eat the seeds from your hand.

Don't try to catch hold of your gerbils though at this stage, instead talk gently and repeat your pets name in a soft tone.

30. Hold me close

They will quickly feel comfortable with your moving your hand around in their cage and soon you'll find that you can gently give them a nose rub.

Lots of gerbils love to have their foreheads and noses rubbed, closing their eyes in pleasure.

Once you've gained their trust it's possible to create the same conditions as a little cave using both hands held close to your body. Some gerbils will find this the perfect conditions to fall asleep.

Top tips

Bites

If he bites, its because he is frightened.

To avoid being bitten, follow these guidelines:

→ Don't pick your gerbils up when while asleep.

→ Talk quietly to your gerbils so that he becomes aware of your presence.

→ Always wash your hands before and after holding them.

→ Remember to keep movements slow and gentle.

✔

31. Friends

Around two weeks later, your gerbil should love being held and be very friendly.

Even with responsible, gentle children, it is recommended they do not handle the gerbils until you are confident that the gerbils are tame. This avoids a bad early experience, and it is easier and faster to tame gerbils when only one person is working with them. Once they are used to human contact, the children can gradually begin to play with them.

32. Sociable

Your gerbil is a very social animal and unlike the solitary _Syrian_ hamster, it won't like being alone.

If you're planning on getting gerbils as pets, you should get at least two. Single gerbils won't be happy without a friend. They could get overweight and live shorter, less satisfying lives. A lonely gerbil will be less friendly towards you and will be a lot harder to tame. Even with constant attention from their owner it won't make up for the companionship that they would get from a fellow gerbil. They will have to sleep alone, eat alone and won't have anyone to groom them. This will effect their all round happiness and as such it is essential to get them a companion.

Know your gerbil

33. Active & curious

Gerbils are active and inquisitive little animals.

They are busy little explorers that spend much of their time running around their cage, searching and exploring. This comes from their natural instinct to go looking for food. After cleaning the cage, leave a few small pieces of food in an unusual place for your gerbils to find. They will love this hunting game.

Try to change your gerbils surroundings as often as possible. Each new toy or object will give them something interesting to explore.

Even though gerbils are naturally scared of open spaces, a play pen with cardboard boxes, willow sticks and plastic pots will create an adventure playground. Tubes, piles of small logs and the occasional hidden treat will give them places to search, play and rest. The larger environment they have, the better (*supervision is important as they may quickly chew through a cardboard fortress!*).

Edible fun

These are in fact edible houses for your gerbil (*as also featured on p16*). Available from most reputable pet stores they give your gerbil a great place to hide/ sleep as well as munch on if they're feeling lazy.

(as also featured on p16)

Top tips

Markings

Your gerbil's stomach has a small patch of bare skin which is where the scent gland is located. The oily secretion from this gland is used to mark their territory and family members.

They do this by rubbing their bellies against the other gerbil or by mounting them.

Emergency symptoms

If your gerbil displays any of the following signs of illness, immediate veterinary care is needed:

→ **Refusing to eat or drink**
→ **Runny nose***
→ **Labored breathing**
→ **Reluctance to move**
→ **Inability to defecate**
→ **Congestion**

* A runny nose can be caused by an allergic reaction to bedding. Change it as soon as you can.

34. Know your gerbils behavior

→ **Thumping**

There are two reasons gerbils thump:
- → To warn other gerbils in their colony of danger.
- → In times of sexual excitement.

In times of danger or excitement, gerbils will often thump their hind legs on the ground. In the wild, the first gerbil to sense danger will thump their feet to warn the rest of the group. Others will perk up their ears to listen to the warning. Some gerbils will also do this when sexually excited.

→ **Grooming**

Grooming is a vital part of gerbil life. They groom each other both to keep clean and as a way of building social relationships. All gerbils, not just adult pairs, will groom each other. This is a good sign that the group of gerbils are getting along well.

→ **Fighting**

Fighting can take two forms: play fighting and serious fighting. Play fighting is frequent among gerbils, especially pups.

Play fighting is often referred to as *'roughhousing'.* They jump on each other and chase one another around the cage.

Serious fighting sometimes occurs and is much more dangerous. It should be stopped safely and immediately *(see 'Top tips' on p13).*

NEVER bring a lone gerbil to an already established group. If two gerbils are apart for an extended period you may find that they forget each other and will need to put them in separate cages.

→ **Digging madly in the corner**

A digging gerbil is a happy gerbil! Digging in the corner is not an attempt to escape, but something known as *'stereotyped digging'.* It comes from the gerbils natural instinct to dig and is absolutely normal behavior.

Breeding advice

35. Golden rules of breeding

→ **Make sure that you have a home for the litter**

Gerbils are prolific breeders and can have litters as often as every 6-8 weeks. Make sure that you know what you are going to do with them if you are not keeping them. See if there are other breeders in your area. It is unlikely that your pet shop will want them all.

→ **Do you have the time and money? Breeding is rarely a profitable hobby.**

To breed, you will need several cages and equipment for each. You may need to pay vets bills if the animals become ill.

→ **Why are you breeding?**

Think about your goals before you begin. What are you trying to achieve from breeding? Are you looking to breed a certain personality or color?

→ **Do your research**

Read up on breeding. Speak to other breeders to build up your knowledge. Research food, behavior, illnesses and infections. The more you know the better.

36. Selecting a breeding pair

Selection is one of the most vital parts of breeding. Ensure that your pair are unrelated. It is a good idea to source your gerbils from two different backgrounds.

Find a pair that are healthy and have the characteristics that you are looking for in your litter. Consider their personality and color. It is best to only have one pair in the cage as more can lead to fighting and endanger the babies.

37. Preparing the cage

Keep things simple. When preparing a cage, make sure that it is clean and safe for the young pups.

Young only need to be provided wood shavings, bedding to sleep in, food and water. Remove any large objects, wheels or anything else that could fall on or trap your young gerbils. Try to avoid shavings made from cedar or pine as the oils in the wood can cause respiratory problems in pups. Also avoid dust baths in the first 6 weeks as the dust can also cause problems.

38. Introductions (breeding or same sex)

Gerbils aged less than 2 months can normally be introduced without any problems, as can a solitary male with a female less than 2 months. Older gerbils may need a period of segregation to become used to each other.

The cage can be split with fine wire mesh. Just make sure they cannot get to each other. You need to swap them to each others side regularly until they are used to each others scent. When they become relaxed they will stop marking their scent after each swap. This can take up to 2 weeks, so be patient.

When you do put them together, watch for several hours and be ready to part them if they show signs of aggression.

39. Breeding summary

Breeding can be a great experience. However, it is not something to taken on by the novice. Research is vital to success.

Remember to take time to think things over before deciding to breed your gerbils. Once you know the answers to our *'Golden rules of breeding',* you are in a position to try.

Titles in series

 **the kitten**
Top tips for a happy healthy pet

 **the goldfish**
Top tips for a happy healthy pet

 **the rabbit**
Top tips for a happy healthy pet

 **the hamster**
Top tips for a happy healthy pet

 **the gerbil**
Top tips for a happy healthy pet

 **the dwarf rabbit**
Top tips for a happy healthy pet

 **the puppy**
Top tips for a happy healthy pet

 **the guinea pig**
Top tips for a happy healthy pet

 **the dwarf hamster**
Top tips for a happy healthy pet

 **the degu**
Top tips for a happy healthy pet

Copyright © 2013 Magnet & Steel Ltd
Publisher: Magnet & Steel Ltd
Printed and bound in China by PRINTWORKS Int. Ltd.

 **magnet & steel**

Magnet & Steel Ltd
Unit 6
Vale Business Park,
Llandow, United Kingdom. CF71 7PF
sales@magnetsteel.com
www.magnetsteel.com

Sefyll
yn y
Bwlch

Brwydr Llangyndeyrn 1960–1965

W. M. REES

CL